How Can I Deal With...

My Stepfamily

Sally Hewitt

A+

Smart Apple Media

Smart Apple Media is published by
Black Rabbit Books
P.O. Box 3263, Mankato, Minnesota 56002

Printed in the United States

Published by arrangement with the Watts
Publishing Group Ltd, London.

Library of Congress Cataloging-in-
Publication Data

Hewitt, Sally.
    My stepfamily / Sally Hewitt.
    p. cm.—(Smart Apple Media. How can
I deal with—)
    Summary: "Case studies and helpful
advice for kids who have stepparents or
stepsiblings"—Provided by publisher.
    Includes bibliographical references and
index.
    ISBN 978-1-59920-229-7
    1. Stepfamilies—Juvenile literature. 2.
Children of divorced parents—Juvenile
literature. 3. Children of divorced
parents—Family relationships—Juvenile
literature. 4. Stepchildren—Juvenile
literature. 5. Parent and child—Juvenile
literature. I. Title.
HQ759.92.H48 2009
306.874'7—dc22
                            2007035712

Picture credits: John Birdsall/John
Birdsall Photography: 8,18. Bob
Daemmrich/Image Works/Topfoto: 16.
Colin Edwards/Photofusion: 17. Sarah
Flanagan/Photofusion: 9. Spencer
Grant/Art Directors: 21. Ute
Kaphake/Photofusion: 6, 10.
Keystone/Topfoto: 25. Charlotte
Macpherson/Photofusion/Alamy: 22.
David Montford/Photofusion: 11.
Joanne O'Brien/Photofusion: 7. Ulrike
Preuss/Photofusion:front cover main, 5,
15, 26. Anders Ryman/Alamy: 20. Ellen
Senisi/Imageworks/Topfoto: 28. Christa
Stadtler/Photofusion: 12, 13, 14.

Series editor: Sarah Peutrill
Art director: Jonathan Hair
Design: Susi Martin
Picture research: Diana Morris
Series advisor: Sharon Lunney

**Please note: Some of the photos in
this book are posed by models. All
characters, situations and stories
are fictitious. Any resemblance to
real persons, living or dead, is
purely coincidental.**

9 8 7 6 5 4 3 2 1

Contents

What Is a Stepfamily?

If your mom or dad is living with a new partner or has married again, they make a new family called a stepfamily.

A stepfamily can be small—just you and your mom or dad plus your stepmom or dad. It can be big with lots of stepsisters and stepbrothers.

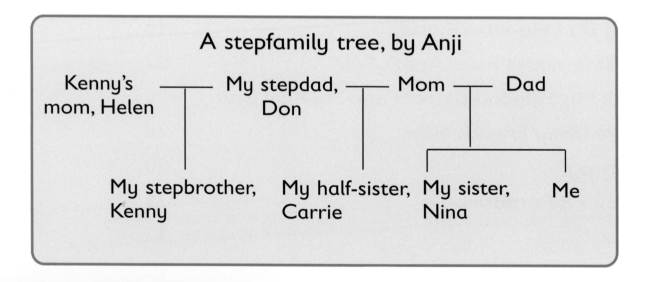

A stepfamily tree, by Anji

Kenny's mom, Helen — My stepdad, Don — Mom — Dad

My stepbrother, Kenny

My half-sister, Carrie

My sister, Nina

Me

You might have two moms—your own mom and your stepmom. You might have two dads, like Anji—your own dad and your stepdad.

Anji's Story

I am part of a stepfamily. When Mom and Dad got divorced, my sister Nina and I stayed with our mom. Then Mom got married again. Her new husband, Don, is our stepdad. Don's son Kenny came to live with us. He's our stepbrother. So **our** mom is Kenny's stepmom! Baby Carrie is Mom and Don's baby. We all think she is really sweet!

Everything's Changing!

Jamie and his dad have been on their own for a long time. Now his dad's partner Gilly and her two children are moving in. Jamie doesn't want things to change.

Jamie's Story

Dad and I are happy together. I like the way we do things. I don't mind seeing Gilly and her children sometimes, but I don't want them living here all the time. I don't see why things have to change.

What Can Jamie Do?

He can:

✔ talk to his dad and say he is worried about Gilly and the children being there all the time, and

✔ ask if he and his dad will still have time together.

What Jamie Did

I told Dad I like it when it's just him and me at home. I don't want things to change. Dad said he loves me, but he loves Gilly too. He wants to be with her as well as with me.

He promises we will still have time together—just him and me. I suppose I'll get used to sharing my Dad.

My Stepdad's Not My Real Dad

Nicky's mom has married again and Nicky is having trouble accepting his new stepdad. He loves his own dad. He doesn't want another dad.

Will's Story

Nicky is my friend. My mom and dad like having him over. He's always nice and polite to them. He even clears away his plate after supper! But he's different at his home. He's really rude to his stepdad.

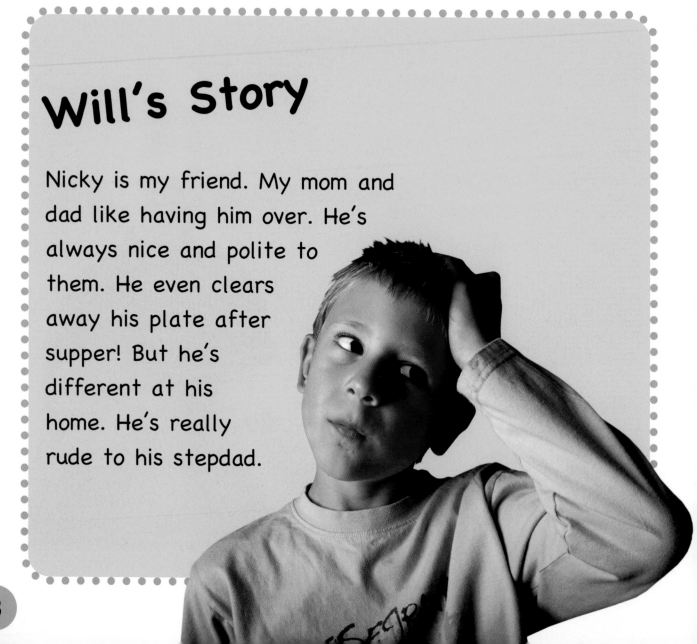

Nicky's Story

Geoff is only my stepdad. He's not my real dad. But Geoff wants me to call him "Dad." Well, I won't! The only person I'll ever call "Dad" is my real dad.

Geoff thinks he can boss me around and tell me what to do! I hope if I'm disobedient and rude to him, he'll get fed up and go away. I'm afraid if I'm nice to him, he might stay. So I'm not nice to him, and I don't call him anything.

What Can Nicky Do?

He can:

✔ remember his stepdad loves his mom, and she would be unhappy if Geoff went away, and

✔ ask if he can call his stepdad "Geoff," and

✔ start to be polite to Geoff and treat him with respect.

What Nicky Did

I know being rude to Geoff makes Mom mad so

I have started to be more polite to him. I've even started doing what I'm told! Now, Geoff and I get along much better.

He doesn't mind me calling him "Geoff" instead of "Dad." Mom is much happier now.

You can love your dad and stepdad in different ways.

A Stepdad's Story

I love Jenny and Sam's mom. I really like Jenny and Sam too. I want us all to be a happy family.

It has been difficult because they love their dad. They were afraid I wanted to take their dad's place. They didn't want to like me.

Now they know I don't want them to stop loving their dad. I just want them to like me, too. We are getting used to our new stepfamily. It's getting better all the time.

Will My Stepmom Stay with Us?

Cherry's dad has a new partner, Jane. He says Jane is going to be Cherry's new stepmother. But Cherry is worried that Jane won't stay with them for long.

Cherry's Story

My dad's ex-partner Emma lived with us for a long time. She was my stepmom and I really liked her. I was sad when she and Dad split up. Now I'm worried my new stepmom will leave us, too. I'm starting to like her a lot already.

What Can Cherry Do?

She can:

✔ tell her dad she is afraid her new stepmom will leave,

✔ ask how she can know Jane will stay and explain she felt sad when Emma left, or

✔ say she doesn't want to feel sad like that again.

What Cherry Did

I told Dad how sad I was when Emma left. I cried and cried. I said, "How do I know Jane won't leave too?"

But Dad said, "Jane and I are getting married." I'm going to be a bridesmaid! Now I know they both really want to stay together for a long time.

I Feel Left Out

Elliot is an only child. Now he has a new stepbrother and stepsister who play together all the time. This makes him feel left out.

David's Story

I'm an only child, the same as my friend Elliot. It can be lonely at home sometimes. I wish I had a new stepbrother and stepsister like Elliot. But he said he feels lonelier than before!

Elliot's Story

My stepbrother and stepsister are used to playing together. They have lots of fun, but they don't ask me to join in their games. They whisper and have secrets with each other.

I think my mom spoils them. She doesn't make them eat their vegetables and she even cleans their bedroom for them! I have to eat all my vegetables and clean my own room. I think Mom loves them more than she loves me. I feel left out.

What Can Elliot Do?

He can talk to his mom and:

✔ tell her that he feels that she loves his stepbrother and stepsister more than him,

✔ tell her she seems to have easier rules for them than for him, and

✔ explain that he feels lonely and left out.

What Elliot Did

I told Mom how I felt. She said she would try to be more fair. Mom plays cards and games with us all and we have fun together. I play with my stepbrother and stepsister without Mom now. Most days, Mom makes sure we spend time together—just Mom and me. I don't feel left out anymore.

Amy also felt left out when she got new stepsisters.

A Mom's Story

When I got married again, my daughter Amy had a new stepdad and two stepsisters. I thought it would nice for her to have someone to play with. But Amy's stepsisters played together and Amy said she felt left out. Her stepsisters said Amy wouldn't join in their games.

So I've started taking them all swimming and they have a great time. Now that they know how much fun they can have together, they are playing together at home, too. Amy and I still have fun together when my stepdaughters visit their mom.

Why Do I Have to Share?

Tilly is used to having a bedroom of her own. Now she has to share her bedroom with her stepsister. But she doesn't want to share it.

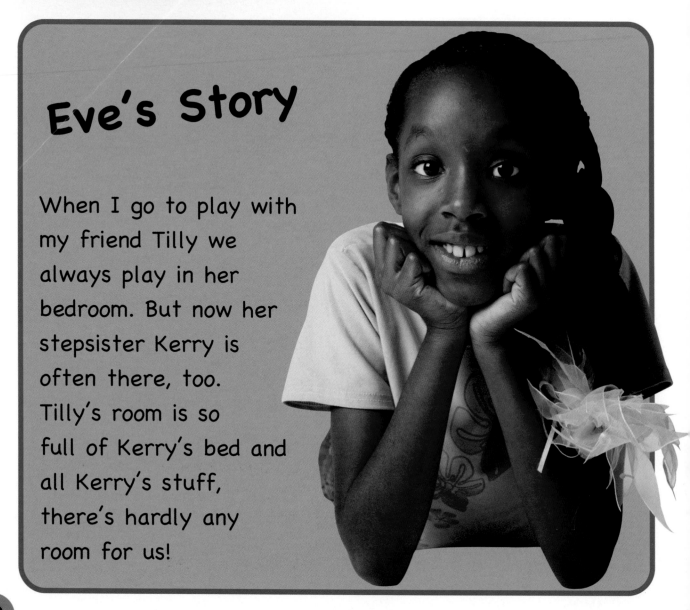

Eve's Story

When I go to play with my friend Tilly we always play in her bedroom. But now her stepsister Kerry is often there, too. Tilly's room is so full of Kerry's bed and all Kerry's stuff, there's hardly any room for us!

Tilly's Story

I used to have my room all to myself. Now I have to share it with my stepsister Kerry. She's older than me. She likes different things. There isn't really enough room for both of us.

When Eve comes over, Kerry's always there so Eve and I play downstairs. But when Kerry has her friends over I *still* have to go downstairs! It's not fair!

Kerry wants a room of her own, and so do I, but there isn't another bedroom in our house.

Tilly's Room STAY OUT!

What Can Tilly Do?

She can:

✔ decide with her stepsister the times they can have the room to themselves,

✔ make their own private spaces in the room, and

✔ remember it's hard for her stepsister to have to share, too.

What Tilly Did

Kerry and I agreed that whoever has a friend over gets the bedroom. Apart from that, I have the bedroom to myself when I get home from school. It's Kerry's after supper. We aren't very clean, but we keep our things on our own sides of the room. Sometimes we like being there together now.

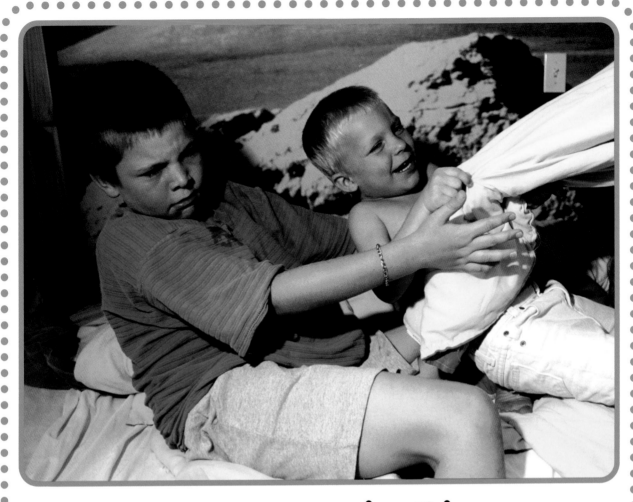

Rory's Story

When Mom and I moved into Mom's partner's house, I had to share a room with his son Benny. Benny's younger than me so we go to bed at different times. If I read with the light on, it wakes Benny up! Then he gets up early and wakes me up! So we fixed up a curtain between our beds. If Benny calls through the curtain, I don't mind. Sometimes I tell him stories if he can't get to sleep.

My Stepmom's Rules Aren't Fair!

Leo doesn't like his stepmom's new rules. He thinks her rules are too strict and that they aren't fair. He argues with her all the time.

Christopher's Story

My friend Leo thinks his stepmom is too strict. I don't think she is really. She only makes the same rules as my mom, like washing the dishes. Leo sticks to my mom's rules without a fuss when he's over at my house.

Leo's Story

My stepmom treats me like a little kid. My stepbrothers are older than me and she sends me to bed earlier than them. She doesn't let me watch the TV shows I want but she lets them watch what they like! When I go to stay with my mom, she lets me stay up late and we watch TV together. We eat chocolate, too, but my stepmom never lets me have chocolate! I argue with my stepmom and I say, "It's not fair! My mom lets me! You can ask my dad."

What Can Leo Do?

He can talk to his dad and stepmom together:

✔ say why he thinks the rules aren't fair

✔ tell them what his mom lets him do

✔ see if they can all agree on some rules

✔ when he has agreed to the rules, try to stick to them without arguing!

What Leo Did

I talked to Dad and my stepmom about rules like my bedtime, washing the dishes, and watching TV.

Now that Dad and I have agreed on the rules with my stepmom, I stick to them—most of the time! When I'm with my mom, she spoils me a bit. That's probably because she doesn't have to put up with me all the time!

Henry also felt he was treated differently than his stepsister.

Henry's Story

My mom always wanted a little girl, but she just had me! When my stepdad's little girl Sarah comes to stay, Mom makes a big fuss over her. She buys her clothes and presents every time she comes! I told Mom I feel like she loves Sarah more than me. Mom gave me a big hug. She said she was sorry and told me how much she loved me.

I don't really mind if she spoils Sarah—as long as she spoils me too sometimes!

I Like My Stepdad Better than My Real Dad

Kyle gets along well with his stepdad. He is worried that his own dad would be unhappy if he knew.

Kyle's Story

I don't look forward to seeing my dad. We don't do anything much. He asks me about what is going on at home. But he gets upset when I tell him! I really like my stepdad. He's good fun, and he makes Mom happy. I feel bad for my dad, but sometimes I think I like my stepdad better.

What Can Kyle Do?

He can:

✔ remember it is all right to love his stepdad,

✔ tell his dad he doesn't want to talk about home with him, or

✔ ask if they can do things together when he sees him.

What Kyle Did

I told Dad I didn't want to talk about home. He said that was okay. I said I wanted to learn Judo on Saturdays. Dad found Judo classes near him. Now we are both learning Judo! It's awesome. We both really enjoy it.

We're Good Friends Now

Aaron and Bonnie are stepbrother and stepsister. They didn't get along with each other at first.

Aaron: When I heard I was going to have a stepsister, I was disappointed. I wanted a stepbrother.

Bonnie: Yeah! And I wanted a stepsister. But I got Aaron!

Aaron: I thought Bonnie would only like girls' stuff—dolls and make-up and pink things.

Bonnie: I thought Aaron would be crazy about soccer and have smelly socks.

Aaron: Actually, I really like riding my bike more than soccer. Bonnie's got a cool bike, too, so we ride our bikes together.

Bonnie: I love reading. Aaron has lots of books and he lends me some. They are great. I lend him my books too. It's like having a whole library at home!

Aaron: Mostly, when Bonnie has her friends over, I keep out of their way. And when I have my friends over, she keeps out of our way.

Bonnie: But we had a great swimming party together for our birthdays. Our friends had a really good time together. So we know our friends get along well if they have to.

Aaron: Bonnie went on vacation with her mom for two weeks and I really missed her.

Bonnie: I thought it would be great to have Aaron out of the way when he visited his Grandma, but I missed him, too.

Aaron: Bonnie and I didn't think we would like each other. But now we are good friends.

Glossary

Divorced
A husband and wife are divorced when they sign papers that mean they are not married anymore.

Fair
A rule is fair when everyone is treated the same way.

Lonely
You are lonely when you don't have many friends and spend a lot of time on your own.

Married
Two people are married when they sign papers that make them husband and wife.

Partners
Two people who live together but are not married are called partners.

Private
You are private when you choose to be alone or keep something to yourself.

Respect
You respect someone when you understand them and are kind to them.

Rules
Rules are things that you must obey. For example:
• bedtime 8 o'clock
• finish homework before watching television.

Share
You share when you tell or give things to other people and you don't keep things to yourself.

Stepfamily
A stepfamily is made when two people who already have children get together to make a new family.

Further Information

For Kids:

http://www.kidshealth.org/kid/feeling/home_family/blended.html

Wondering what to do since your mom or dad got remarried? This site gives you tips on how to live with stepparents.

http://pbskids.org/itsmylife/family/stepfamilies/index.html

Get advice and ideas from experts about living with stepparents, stepbrothers, and stepsisters. Read stories from other kids who have stepfamilies.

http://www.divorcestep.com/kids/index.shtml

This site has a special kids' section with articles and books about being a stepchild, why parents divorce, and more.

For Parents:

http://www.bonusfamilies.com/

Step families are a "bonus," according to this web site, which offers resources for stepfamilies, stepparents, and stepchildren.

http://www.stepfamilies.info/faqs/facts.php

The home page of the National Stepfamily Resource Center offers information and educational resources to stepfamilies.

http://www.newlifeafterdivorce.com/

Articles and tips on parenting, financial issues, health, and relationships, for parents adjusting to life after they get a divorce.

For Teachers:

http://www.teachablemoment.org/toolbox/toughtimestoolbox.html

This site offers tips for addressing tough issues in your classroom and for helping kids express their feelings.

Note to parents and teachers: Every effort has been made by the publishers to ensure that these Web sites are suitable for children, that they are of the highest educational value, and that they contain no inappropriate or offensive material. However, because of the nature of the Internet, it is impossible to guarantee that the contents of these sites will not be altered. We strongly advise that Internet access is supervised by a responsible adult.

Index

Notes for Parents, Caregivers, and Teachers

Some children will enjoy being part of a stepfamily. Others will find it difficult. There are many ways parents, caregivers, and teachers can help children deal with their stepfamily.

• Having a good relationship with their natural parents can help children get along with their stepparents.
• It helps children to know that their dad will always be Dad and their mom will always be Mom whatever happens.
• It helps to have special times alone with your natural child.
• Parents can help by not quizzing their child about what goes on in their stepfamily, although don't avoid talking about it either.

Page 6 Jamie's Story
Jamie doesn't want his dad's partner and her children to move in with them. He wants his dad to himself.
• Talking about feelings and discussing ways to cope can help children to deal with change.

Page 9 Nicky's Story
Nicky doesn't want his stepdad to replace his new dad and is being rude and disobedient.
• Expecting children to behave politely and with respect however they feel and then treating them the same way is a helpful step towards getting along better together.

Page 12 Cherry's Story
Cherry is worried that her new stepmom will leave her and her dad.

• Children are affected by a new relationship and need love and consideration when decisions are being made.

Page 15 Elliot's Story
Elliot thinks his mom favors his stepbrother and stepsister and he feels left out.
• It helps to be fair to every child in a stepfamily and treat them all the same.

Page 19 Tilly's Story
Tilly is finding it difficult to share her bedroom with her older stepsister.
• Agreeing on rules and organizing personal space can help when children have to share a bedroom.

Page 22 Leo's Story
Leo resents his stepmom's rules and thinks she is stricter than his own mom.
• Children can play one parent off the other to get their own way. Rules that are fair and reasonable should be stuck to by parents and children.

Page 26 Kyle's Story
Kyle is worried because he has more fun with his stepdad than with his own dad.
• Planning a shared activity or learning something new together can help build a good relationship with your children if you don't live with them.

Page 28 Aaron and Bonnie's story
Children could role-play the parts in this simple script. They could also write and perform their own play about living in a stepfamily.